D0426914

Praise for
RECLAIMING COMMON SENSE

In the modern intellectual climate, the basic rationality of common sense has been unsettled, and sometimes altogether eclipsed, by dreamworld ideologies and personal "truths" asserted in defiance of elementary facts of experience. The revolt against common sense has moved beyond the universities to take hold of our political and cultural institutions, in coercive government policies and public shaming. Against the feverish assault, Robert Curry sounds a note of cool sanity, presenting common sense in simple (though not simplistic) terms and illustrating it in living color. For level-headed readers disoriented by the craziness, this little book will be a bracing tonic.

SCOTT PHILIP SEGREST

Associate Professor of Political Science at The Citadel
and author of *America and the Political Philosophy of Common Sense*

In his second companion volume about common sense, Robert Curry again reminds us that our leisured and affluent society periodically dismisses the fundamental Western way of knowledge that ensures our collective success. Or at least it says it does in its periodic relativist, romantic, and emotional flirtations with thoughts that are not grounded in reality. This book is a much-needed reminder in our postmodern age that what works and what we perceive to be real are alone real.

VICTOR DAVIS HANSON

Senior Fellow at the Hoover Institution, Stanford University,
and author of *The Second World Wars: How the First Global Conflict Was Fought and Won*

In his entertaining, insightful, and highly literate new book, Robert Curry gives the "superpower" that is common sense its proper due. Here's hoping that members of the political class read Curry's book, and in so doing find within themselves the humble qualities that might cause them to do less so that we the people can do more.

JOHN TAMNY
Vice President of FreedomWorks

What Robert Curry started simply and beautifully in *Common Sense Nation* he continues in *Reclaiming Common Sense*: the revival, defense, and application of the principles needed to save America and Western civilization.

Ryan P. Williams
President of the Claremont Institute
and Publisher of the *Claremont Review of Books*

Having recovered in *Common Sense Nation* the important role of common sense in the nation's founding, Robert Curry has written a thoughtful, passionate analysis of the social and political ills that have followed the abandonment of common sense in our country's culture. From appeasement of jihadism to the follies of self-selected gender identities, Curry provides a powerful, must-read warning of the dangers to our principles of self-government and our political freedom by neglecting "common sense realism" in our policies both at home and abroad.

BRUCE S. THORNTON
Research Fellow at the Hoover Institution, Stanford University

RECLAIMING COMMON SENSE

RECLAIMING COMMON SENSE

Finding Truth in a Post-Truth World

Robert Curry

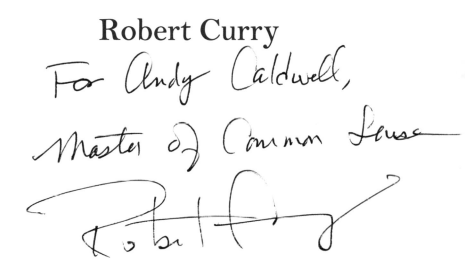

For Andy Caldwell,

Master of Common Sense

Robert Curry

Encounter
BOOKS

NEW YORK · LONDON

First American edition published in 2019 by Encounter Books,
an activity of Encounter for Culture and Education, Inc.,
a nonprofit, tax-exempt corporation.
Encounter Books website address: www.encounterbooks.com

Manufactured in the United States and printed on acid-free paper.
The paper used in this publication meets the minimum requirements of
ANSI/NISO Z39.48 − 1992 (R 1997) (*Permanence of Paper*).

FIRST AMERICAN EDITION

LIBRARY OF CONGRESS CATALOGING-IN-PUBLICATION DATA

Names: Curry, Robert, 1944– author.
Title: Reclaiming Common Sense : finding truth in a post-truth world /
by Robert Curry.
Description: New York : Encounter Books, [2019] |
Includes bibliographical references and index.
Identifiers: LCCN 2019013891 (print) | LCCN 2019980538 (ebook) |
ISBN 9781641770743 (hardcover : alk. paper) |
ISBN 9781641770750 (ebook)
Subjects: LCSH: Common sense.
Classification: LCC B105.C457 C87 2019 (print) |
LCC B105.C457 (ebook) |
DDC 148—dc23
LC record available at https://lccn.loc.gov/2019013891
LC ebook record available at https://lccn.loc.gov/2019980538

To Lisa, my joy

The medium of his thought is common sense, and his commitment to intellect is fortified by an old-fashioned faith that the truth can be got at, that we can, if we actually want to, see the object as it really is.

Lionel Trilling, on George Orwell

Common sense in an uncommon degree is what the world calls wisdom.

Samuel Taylor Coleridge

Say what you want about the liberal arts, but they've found a cure for common sense.

Robert Godwin

CONTENTS

Foreword, by Brian T. Kennedy   13

Prologue   17

The War on Common Sense   23

The Philosopher of Common Sense   29

Knowing and Doing   33

Dreaming   39

Knowing, Doing, and Saying   43

Doing Science   49

Doing Psychotherapy   55

Gaining Self-Mastery   61

Self-Mastery and Self-Rule   71

Rejecting Common Sense   79

Romanticism   87

Imposing an Alternative to Common Sense   95

Misunderstanding Einstein   99

Suggestions for Further Reading   103

Index   105

FOREWORD

At the heart of this wonderful book by Robert Curry is the simple belief that you as a human being can govern yourself. That shouldn't be a controversial proposition, but when an army of federal bureaucrats, university professors, and social science "experts" begin telling you how you ought to be living your life or running your business or raising your children, you might start to wonder. You may begin doubting your own ability to make decisions and to distinguish true from false, with the fundamental faculty of common sense.

For over a century now, there has been a sustained attack on common sense – on what Curry calls the foundation of the American founding. It was the common sense of the American people that led to the American Revolution, the creation and ratification of the Constitution, the vindication of both in a bloody civil war, and the defense of America and the West in the wars of the twentieth century. America was the most successful experiment in liberty and self-government that the world had ever seen. But some people have a different plan for us.

Progressive intellectuals have long been trying to turn the free and self-governing people of the United States into wards of a massive bureaucracy, or what the political philosopher John Marini has called the "administrative state." Many refer to it as Big Government. In order to get Americans to reject self-rule under a limited constitutional government and to accept rule by bureaucrats and "experts" instead, progressives needed first and foremost to undermine people's confidence in their own common sense, and to discredit *moral* common sense too.

As Curry so elegantly explains, common sense is the basis for countless daily choices and actions. We rely on common sense in decisions concerning safety and security, in matters of life or death. We also employ common sense in questions of right and wrong. Common sense is the indispensable starting point for knowing what is true and what is morally right. We simply cannot get along without it.

Then why is common sense now being so badly eroded? This book tells how progressive intellectuals have sought to elevate academic theories and fashions above common sense, and establish their preferred doctrines in its place. They have foisted social science, and later its handmaiden, political correctness, onto the American people in the hope of smothering the exercise of common sense. In large measure, higher education today is a war on common sense. To say this is not to disparage the importance of education. Rather, it is a criticism of the modern university, with its disdain for the belief in truth and its embrace of intellectual and moral relativism. It is a criticism of the intellectual forces that are weakening the influence of common sense in the lives of the American people.

Certainly, most of us still have and use the common sense that prevents us from giving knives to babies or drinking gasoline to quench our thirst. But when it comes to anything involving political issues or social policy, common sense is frowned upon as passé or low-brow – as out of touch with how educated, sophisticated people see things. This message is drummed in so insistently that many average Americans have learned to distrust what their own common sense tells them.

When citizens no longer trust common sense – when they doubt their primary means of distinguishing true from false – they can fall prey to ideologies that are antithetical to self-rule and to human freedom. The misery and carnage brought by totalitarian ideologies in the twentieth century is stark evidence of the danger. We have not yet reached that point in America, but we are terribly close.

That is why this is such an important book. Its purpose is to remind Americans that it is not only acceptable but salutary – indeed, necessary – to guide their lives by common sense, and to use their God-given ability to discern right and wrong, true and false. Common sense is still the surest resource we have for knowing how best to live our lives, and how to live in society with others. The opinions of a thousand PhDs do not make it otherwise.

It is not too late for the American people to recover their confidence in common sense. If they do, they can make America great again. And failure, of course, is not an option.

BRIAN T. KENNEDY
President, The American Strategy Group
Director, The Claremont Institute

PROLOGUE

There was nothing about Ulysses S. Grant that struck the eye; and this puzzled people, after it was all over, because it seemed reasonable that greatness, somewhere along the line, should look like greatness. Grant could never look like anything ... and afterward men could remember nothing more than the fact that when he came around things seemed to happen. The most they could say, usually, was that U. S. Grant had a good deal of common sense.

BRUCE CATTON
Grant Moves South

GENERAL GEORGE MCCLELLAN had failed again and again to solve the problem he faced: how to use the Army of the Potomac to bring the Civil War to a successful conclusion. Everyone — especially McClellan! — knew that McClellan was brilliant. Yet he could not get it done. Then Ulysses S. Grant was given command, and he led the army to victory. The common-sense general did what the brilliant general could not do.

In histories and biographies of the Civil War, it is fascinating to observe authors struggling to reconcile what Grant accomplished with the plainness of the man. In their defense, it must be admitted that there is

17

something unobtrusive about common sense, even in uncommon measure, so it is easily overlooked. But once you begin to examine it, you may be swept away from our everyday world of ordinary people and find yourself looking into profound depths filled with fascinating wonders. I propose that we boldly venture out into the deep.

I have a witty and perspicacious friend who says that common sense is a "superpower." Indeed it is. But it is a superpower we all have in common, even if some of us have it only in the ordinary degree. It is the power that makes us rational beings and moral agents. It enables us to meet the challenges of daily existence as human beings – and also to meet extraordinary challenges, as Ulysses S. Grant did.

Our common-sense superpower is what makes us human. Without it, what would we be? Something strange, certainly.

To get an idea of what our life might be without common sense, let's consider François Truffaut's fascinating film *The Wild Child*. It recounts an idealistic Frenchman's struggle to bring a feral child, a boy who grew up in the wild without human contact, into the human community. Because the boy did not grow up among people, he had only the physical attributes of humankind. He looked like a boy, but he lacked the other traits that a boy his age would normally have. He was biologically a boy, but he had never developed the superpower we all take for granted. Consequently, the effort to make a boy of him had to begin with the kind of training we use with our pets.

The story of the wild child makes this clear: while our capacity for common sense is inborn, we must enter into the common life of a human community to develop it. If we are deprived of the opportunity to participate in the shared life of people who have cultivated the superpower we have in common, that capacity is unrealized. In this respect it is like language. We have an innate capacity for language, features of which are apparently hardwired in our nervous system, but we learn to speak only by interaction with other people.

Between the feral boy and the Zen-like mystery that was Ulysses S. Grant, there is an enormous distance, and most of us live somewhere in between. We all have the capacity for common sense, and most of us employ it in our daily lives. In fact, we cannot get along without it. Common sense is the foundation of thinking and of human action. And yet it has long been under attack by intellectual and cultural elites, who tell us to mistrust what it teaches us. That is the reason for this little book.

THIS IS MY second book with the term "common sense" in the title. The two books are related but not similar. The first one, *Common Sense Nation*, explores the thinking of the American Founders. Its focus is the pattern of ideas that connects the Declaration of Independence and the Constitution of the United States. My aim in that book was to present to Americans today what was once known by virtually every American. For a century or more after the Revolutionary War, the common-sense thinking of the Founders was studied and taught in American colleges, and its precepts – both practical and moral – pervaded American society. It was the coin of the realm in American thought. This fact of our history has been forgotten to an astonishing degree.

For the last century or more, there has been a concerted effort to delegitimize the American founding. That campaign originated on American university campuses but now has spread throughout the culture. Today, elite opinion in America assumes that the founding was deeply flawed, that the Founders' ideas are outmoded, and that the system they designed needs to be fundamentally transformed. This is well known. What is not so much recognized is the connection between that campaign and the campaign to delegitimize common sense that has been going on at the same time.

The war on common sense is an attack on the foundation of the American founding. An effort to restore the American idea therefore faces a double challenge. While *Common Sense Nation* addresses the challenge to the American founding by presenting anew the Founders' understanding of what they were establishing, *Reclaiming Common Sense* takes up the other challenge: the challenge to the foundation of the founding.

The unrelenting attacks on common sense have created something truly strange: a widespread notion that we have somehow moved beyond common sense, even though we still inescapably live and move and act in the realm of common sense in our every waking moment. This book exposes the absurdity of those attacks and draws upon well-known stories from the Western literary tradition to help us regain our footing in common sense. My goal is to restore a trust in common sense and an understanding of its crucial role in our lives. I aim to inspire confidence in your own common sense, which I hope will be helpful to you in your personal life and in your role as an American citizen.

THE WAR ON COMMON SENSE

State a moral case to a ploughman and a professor. The former will decide it as well and often better than the latter, because he has not been led astray by artificial rules.

THOMAS JEFFERSON

WHEN THOMAS PAINE appealed to "common sense" to make the case for American independence, it probably never crossed his mind that there would ever be a need to make the case for common sense itself, at least not in America. But common-sense thinking has fallen out of favor. Because it has been under attack for a very long time, it no longer gets the respect it once commanded. Deep thinkers have discarded it, elites have learned to disdain it, and many of us have had our confidence in its value badly shaken.

The consequences are enormous. Faltering belief in common sense is behind the rejection of the Founders' idea of America. More broadly, it is behind the astonishing rejection of Western civilization by its own people – a rejection that has reached what looks to be a civilization-ending crisis in Europe.

Examples of the war on common sense are now everywhere in public life. How about the denial of the plain fact that humans are either male or female? Not long ago, a boy in a tutu and a tiara who claimed he was a girl would still be regarded as a boy. Today, academic and cultural elites as well as government officials insist that "gender identity" is more real than biology. They say there are many genders, and one website tells me there are *sixty-three*. Elites tell us we had better get with the many-gender program, or else. And while we are at it, we had better get politically correct about marriage. We are told that marriage no longer means one thing, a union between a man and a woman. How long will it be until we have sixty-three varieties of marriage?

The war on moral common sense has reached new heights of absurdity. If we point out a need for common-sense steps to protect ourselves from Islamic terrorists, we are said to suffer a psychological condition called "Islamophobia." But unlike other phobias, such as claustrophobia, this condition is said to make us victimizers rather than victims. Similarly, if we say that America needs to secure its borders, we are met by cries that "walls are immoral." Evidently the common-sense wisdom that good walls make good neighbors has been taken down by the masters of political correctness.

Political correctness is quite simply a war on common sense. It is a war by the elites on the common people and on the shared understanding of basic realities of life that has made it possible for us to rule ourselves under the Constitution. Once this common-sense understanding of reality has been vanquished, it is "mission accomplished" for the Americans who reject America.

The Founders realized that there might eventually come a time when their achievement was no longer understood – when perhaps one generation simply failed to pass the understanding on to the next. But the possibility that common sense could be abandoned to the extent it is today would most likely have been beyond their imagining. And no wonder, for a great deal of effort has gone into assailing it. Proponents of irrationalist doctrines that came on in wave after wave beginning in the nineteenth century – romanticism, Hegelianism, Marxism, progressivism, existentialism, postmodernism, and the like – have been pounding away at common sense for a very long time.

ONCE UPON A TIME, the foundation of an American college education was common sense. The philosophy that young Americans learned in college was called common-sense realism, a philosophy that was "virtually the official creed of the American Republic," in the words of the great American historian Arthur Herman. Another great historian, Allen Guelzo, in his lecture series titled "The American Mind," notes that prior to the Civil War, "every major [American] collegiate intellectual" subscribed to that philosophy.

According to Guelzo, most American professors continued to be common-sense realists until a revolution in academia around the beginning of the twentieth century pushed them out. The result was the end of an academic tradition that reached back to the founding era, a tradition which had meant learning to think like an American. The central role of common-sense realism in the American tradition is today unknown to most Americans –

which is testimony to the astonishing success and thoroughness of that campus revolution.

As you know, we have had another revolution on campus since then. The student revolution of the 1960s eventually resulted in populating American colleges with politically radicalized professors who veered even further from the tradition of common-sense realism. In the 1960s it was still possible to get a real education on campus if you made the effort, though common-sense realism was nowhere to be found in the curriculum. But if you have followed what has been happening at your alma mater or elsewhere in academia, you already know that education has been replaced by indoctrination in multiculturalism and an ever-changing array of politically correct doctrines that are inimical to the American foundational philosophy.

This, in outline, is the story of how we now have so many Americans who reject America.

B ECAUSE WE NO LONGER learn about the philosophy of common-sense realism that once marked the education of America's elite, let's begin with how Arthur Herman defines it:

The power of common judgment belongs to everyone, rich or poor, educated or uneducated; indeed, we exercise it every day in hundreds of ways. Of course, ordinary people make mistakes — but so do philosophers. And sometimes they cannot prove what they believe is true, but many phi-

losophers have the same problem. On some things, however, like the existence of the real world and basic moral truths, they know they don't have to prove it. These things are ... self-evident, meaning they are "no sooner understood than they are believed" because they "carry the light of truth itself."

The core idea of common-sense realism is that there are self-evident truths – truths which do not need to be proved. Self-evident truths are the foundation of human understanding; they are the necessary basis for knowing anything at all. We know self-evident truths by means of our common sense.

Does that phrase "self-evident truths" ring a bell? Yes, it echoes the familiar line from the Declaration of Independence. When Jefferson and the other Founders wrote "We hold these truths to be self-evident," they revealed their reliance on the philosophy of common-sense realism.

Abraham Lincoln vividly expressed the same philosophy when he asked: "If you call a tail a leg, how many legs would a dog have?" The answer: "Four, because even if you call it a leg, it's still a tail." Of course, this is ordinary common sense. In Lincoln's time, the dominant philosophy taught in American colleges was deeply rooted in the common-sense thinking of ordinary Americans. Under the same philosophy, if a boy calls himself a girl, he is still a boy.

The powerful affinity between the thinking of ordinary Americans and the common-sense realism of those who constituted America's educated elite explains why in former times they understood each other. It also explains why the Founders believed that Americans could govern themselves: they had faith in the common sense of ordinary people.

Ordinary Americans, for the most part, are still common-sense realists, even if they have never heard of the formal philosophy, and especially if they have never been to college. But the intellectual affinity with cultural and political elites has been lost. Elites and average people no longer understand each other, and our colleges and universities are teaching students to distrust their own common sense and to deny the existence of objective truth.

When someone today dares to use the word "truth," many have been conditioned to respond by asking "Whose truth?" And so the discussion ends. We are being told that there are no basic moral truths, that there are really no truths at all, only the prevailing tenets of multiculturalism and political correctness. These doctrines, if accepted, deprive Americans of the ability to carry out their responsibilities as citizens – in voting, in serving on a jury, and in their community lives. Undermining the very concepts of truth and common sense accomplishes quite a lot for the enemies of the American system of liberty that is the gift of the Founders.

THE PHILOSOPHER OF
COMMON SENSE

If there are certain principles, as I think there are, which the constitution of our nature leads us to believe, and which we are under a necessity to take for granted in the common concerns of life, without being able to give a reason for them; these are what we call the principles of common sense; and what is manifestly contrary to them, is what we call absurd.

THOMAS REID
*An Inquiry into the Human Mind
on the Principles of Common Sense*

A BRIEF VISIT with the founding father of the philosophy of common sense will help us get our bearings as we explore the fascinating subject of common sense.

Thomas Reid was Professor of Moral Philosophy at the University of Glasgow, and he referred to his philosophical method as "common sense realism." He published his great work, *An Inquiry into the Human Mind on the Principles of Common Sense,* in 1764. It is difficult to overstate his importance to the American founding. As we have seen, Arthur Herman emphasizes this point, writing that "Common Sense Realism was virtually the official creed of the American Republic."

Reid's philosophical purpose was to provide a foundation for morality and for knowledge. He argued that there is an endowment of human nature that makes both morality and knowledge possible, and he called it common sense. Because we possess it, we human beings can master speech, geometry, ship building, and a host of other skills that are unique to humankind. It enables us to serve on a jury and weigh the evidence presented in a trial. With it we are able to make rational judgments and moral judgments. Common sense is the human attribute that makes it possible for us to be rational creatures and moral agents.

Reid's fundamental insight was that our ability to make sense of our experience presupposes certain first principles. Because these principles are implicit in our conduct and our thought, they cannot be proved; there are no other truths from which they can be derived. However, to deny or even to doubt any of them is to involve ourselves in absurdity. Consequently, the principles of common sense have the special authority of first principles: we cannot operate without them. They are inarguably true and "self-evident." In Reid's words (which we have seen quoted by Herman), common-sense judgments are "no sooner understood than they are believed," because they "carry the light of truth itself."

Whatever is contrary to the principles of common sense is, in Reid's term, "absurd." Let's examine that word. According to *Roget's Thesaurus*, its synonyms are "ridiculous, ludicrous, laughable, silly, preposterous, foolish, outrageous, asinine, idiotic, loony, stupid, crazy, nonsense." No doubt "nonsense" is the one that best captures Reid's meaning. To reject the self-evident principles of common sense, then, is to indulge in nonsense.

As you know, the American Founders claimed they were guided by self-evident truths. They relied on self-evident truths because their deliberations were deeply informed by the thinking of Thomas Reid. And Reid continued to be at the center of American thought for more than a century. Generations of American academics were common-sense realists, and as noted earlier, Allen Guelzo points out that until the Civil War, every major American collegiate intellectual was a common-sense realist.

Reid is all but forgotten in America today. He is routinely missing from survey courses in philosophy and even from courses in American thought. You may very well have never heard of him. But you don't have to read his *Inquiry into the Human Mind on the Principles of Common Sense* to understand common sense. You already have everything you need for that.

KNOWING AND DOING

Giving money and power to government is like giving whiskey and car keys to teenage boys.

P. J. O'ROURKE
Parliament of Whores

COMMON SENSE IS most familiar to us as our shared understanding of the way things are. But perhaps we understand it best when we consider its absence, and when we agree on what "makes no sense."

It is easy to see that P. J. O'Rourke is making an argument from common sense in the statement above, by appealing to a shared understanding of what is nonsensical. We all know that we shouldn't give car keys and whiskey to teenage boys. How do we know? Ask anyone and they are likely to say, "It's just common sense."

Our common sense gives us the implicit major premise of a syllogism, with the quotation above being the minor premise. Put them together, and here is the argument:

A. Giving whiskey and car keys to teenage boys is dangerous and unwise.

B. Giving money and power to government is like giving whiskey and power to teenage boys.

C. Therefore, giving money and power to government is dangerous and unwise.

Of course, you may not buy the conclusion. But if you see no danger in giving money and power to government, you are not likely to attack the argument at A, which for all practical purposes is unassailable. If you are going to attack the argument, you will surely strike at B, and insist that giving money and power to government is completely different from giving whiskey and car keys to teenage boys. You wouldn't get very far by attacking A, because A is common sense. Disputing A is a losing strategy because we – you and I – believe that A is *true*.

Granted, there are sophisticated people who deny that there is any such thing as truth. You may even be one of those sophisticated people yourself. (If you are, I want to thank you for reading this far. Please continue!) But no matter how strongly those sophisticated people insist there is no such thing as truth, they can generally be counted on not to provide teenage boys with whiskey and car keys. They also won't let their infant children play with sharp knives. They aren't going to jump into the Grand Canyon holding an umbrella to find out whether doing so would get them safely to the bottom. In their actions they honor common-sense truth.

The truths of common sense can be stated, but they usually don't need to be, and consequently are seldom stated at all. They are demonstrated in what we do and what we refrain from doing. They are revealed in every action we take, especially when we do something that displays a lack of common sense.

We are able to state the truths of common sense because we live those truths – and the ability to live the truths of common sense makes a human life possible. It is therefore about as precious as human life itself. We are made aware of this whenever we witness the heart-breaking struggles of those who are in the process of losing their access to the world of common sense, such as victims of Alzheimer's disease. Their ability to participate in the human world we share and their ability to take care of themselves diminish toward a vanishing point as their disease robs them of the common sense we take for granted.

Even people who are normally of sound mind can temporarily lose access to the world of common sense and find themselves in a strange and unfamiliar world. I experienced this firsthand when I visited a friend who was recovering from a prolonged period in a coma. He had undergone several major surgeries, and he was being administered an astonishing number of medications of all types. Though he was able to recognize me, he did not understand that he was in a hospital. This had caused constant problems for the nurses and staff. He begged me to help him escape from "this place where they are keeping me prisoner." He told me he had met with the president in the Oval Office the day before and that the president would help us escape if only I would call the White House. I briefly tried to get him to understand that he was in a hospital, but soon abandoned the attempt. Bizarre, frightening, absurd stories of what had been happening poured out of him. His loss of common sense made conversation impossible. All I could offer him was the reassurance of a familiar face.

Understanding this aspect of common sense can take us to the very foundations of what we know and how we know. Consider, for example, cases of the most severe psychiatric disorders. When a person is incapable of functioning at a necessary minimum level of common sense, we say that person is insane.

Imagine that a patient in a psychiatric hospital tells you he is Napoleon Bonaparte or that the hospital attendants are actually disguised Mafia assassins out to get him. You do not alert the French embassy or call the police. Why not? No matter how sincere the patient is, your common-sense knowledge of the world lets you know not to take his claims at face value. The patient's problem is not the Mafia or other people's failure to recognize that he is the Emperor of the French. The problem is that the patient has lost contact with reality.

"Lost contact with reality." Think about that phrase for a moment. To have common sense is to be in meaningful contact with the human reality we have in common. Just as our eyes reveal to us the visual world, common sense reveals to us the world of human understanding and action. In this respect, common sense functions like our other senses. No wonder we call it a "sense."

It is easy to overlook common sense for the same reason. We think about what our senses reveal to us, but give little thought to the means by which those things are revealed. Likewise, we are caught up in our experience of the world of common sense, and we don't notice the means by which we are able to apprehend it.

So, common sense is absolutely fundamental to our ability to live as human beings, yet it is easy to overlook. The ideal way for us to understand the role of common sense in our lives would be to experience life without it for ourselves. If only we had access to such an experience! It would enable us to see vividly how common sense makes our world.

Actually, we do have access to such an experience.

DREAMING

Stiva ... opened his eyes. "Yes, yes, how did it go?" he thought, recalling his dream. "Yes! Alabin was giving a dinner in Darmstatdt — no, not in Darmstadt but something American. Yes, but this Darmstadt was in America. Yes, Alabin was giving a dinner on glass tables, yes — and the tables were singing Il mio Tesoro, *only it wasn't* Il mio Tesoro *but something better, and there were some little carafes, which were also women," he recalled. His eyes glittered merrily, and he fell to thinking with a smile. "Yes, it was nice, very nice. There were many other excellent things there, but one can't say it in words, or even put it into waking thoughts."*

LEO TOLSTOY
Anna Karenina

We find ourselves in a different world when we dream. Common-sense rules do not apply there. Tables can sing arias from Mozart operas, and little carafes can somehow at the same time be women. The German city of Darmstadt can somehow also be in America. In our dreams we can fly through the air or interact with friends and family who have died. People, objects, and places change unaccountably into other people, objects, and places, or are somehow both at once. One moment we are in one locale and then we are in another without having covered the intervening distance, or we are somehow in both places at the same time. And so on *ad infinitum.*

The world of the dream is our world absent the principles of common sense.

In the daily cycle of waking, dreaming, and sleeping, we experience the most basic truth about the nature of human reality. Awake, we live in the common-sense world of our shared experience. Dreaming, we inhabit a world lacking the truths of common sense and shared experience. And in the unconsciousness of dreamless sleep, we disappear and the world disappears also. "When you are filled with sleep, you never were," says Darl Bundren in William Faulkner's *As I Lay Dying.*

In this daily cycle we know two very different worlds by means of two different states of consciousness: in waking consciousness we exist and act in the common-sense world of our common experience; in the dream state we find ourselves in a world where the common-sense rules of our shared experience do not apply.

We know each other in the common-sense world. There we all meet: the foolish, deficient in common sense; the ideologues and fanatics, who sacrifice common sense on the altar of their beliefs; the wise, with their uncommon degree of common sense; and all the rest of us.

Comparing the dream world with the world of waking consciousness – the common-sense world of our common experience – enables us to realize that there is a level of common-sense truth even deeper than that of P. J. O'Rourke's maxim about teenagers and whiskey.

People who possess common sense would agree that it is *unwise* to give whiskey and car keys to teenagers, or sharp knives to babies. But if they are told that tables can sing operatic arias and that little carafes can also be women, they would say it's *absurd*. Those propositions are a more serious affront to common sense.

If you insist that the carafes on the table are also women, you are inviting a psychiatric evaluation. If you insist that you can fly through the air if you jump out of a window, and look ready to act upon that belief, it would generally be understood that you are putting your life at grave risk. Common sense at this level is the foundation of the possibility for a shared understanding of the way things really are, of how we can do things together, and even of what is necessary for our survival.

At this level, common-sense truths have a certainty beyond any possible challenge. There is no need to prove that tables can't sing or that carafes cannot at the same time be women. These are truths that require no proof. To use the language favored by Thomas Reid and the American Founders, these common-sense truths are "self-evident." Understanding self-evident truths is necessary for understanding anything else at all.

KNOWING, DOING, AND SAYING

There is much greater similitude than is commonly imag-
ined, between the testimony of nature given by our senses,
and the testimony of men given by language.

Thomas Reid
An Inquiry into the Human Mind
on the Principles of Common Sense

The principles of the world of common sense are
all there in our language and at the ready. Consequently,
we can articulate the reality revealed by common sense,
the world of our common experience. The common-
sense world is *sayable*.

It is much harder to put the experience of our dreams
into words because the dream world lacks the common-
sense structure we find in the waking world and in our
language. "One can't say it in words, or even put it into
waking thoughts," says Tolstoy's Stiva of his dream.
We find it difficult to recount our dream experiences
because our language grew out of a very different world:
the waking world, which we experience in common and
understand by common sense.

In trying to describe our dreams, we are constantly
required to say how the events diverged from common

sense. Look again at Stiva's account of his dream (emphasis added):

"Yes! Alabin was giving a dinner in Darmstatdt – no, not in Darmstadt but something American. Yes, but this Darmstadt was in America. *Yes, Alabin was giving a dinner on glass tables, yes* – and the tables were singing *Il mio Tesoro,* only it wasn't *Il mio Tesoro* but something better, *and there were some little carafes,* which were also women," *he recalled.*

Note how much of the account deals with deviations from the way things are in the world of common sense. Now imagine a scenario with the same basic structure but without the challenges to common sense. Here is how brief the account would be:

Alabin was giving a dinner in Darmstadt. There were little carafes on glass tables.

We can recount our waking experiences with relative ease, but struggle to fit our dream world into language. That is because human language is common sense in action: putting our thoughts in order and conveying them in a way that *makes sense* to others.

THE SIGNIFICANCE OF the fact that human language grows out of the waking world which we have in common can be missed even by the most intelligent among us. One interesting example of this failure is the most famous pronouncement of the philosopher René Descartes.

Descartes, as is well known, set modern philosophy in motion with his formulation "I think, therefore I am" (*Cogito, ergo sum*). He began from a position of doubting virtually everything, including the existence of the world and other people. He claimed that only his own existence could not be doubted. Then, having arrived at that one certain truth, he set out to prove that the world and other people exist.

But Descartes overlooked the implications of the fact that he was using language to conduct his philosophical inquiry. Language presupposes the existence of other people, in a world that actually exists. I learned American English growing up among speakers of American English, and American English has roots deep in history and prehistory. That I am now writing in American English presupposes all the people I learned it from and all the generations who bequeathed it to them, and the many generations who gradually shaped it out of prior languages. More fundamentally, there would be no such thing as language if not for the human need to communicate with other people. Descartes therefore had unwittingly already assumed what he was attempting to prove.

That the world and other people exist is a common-sense truth, with a certainty beyond any possible challenge. Its truth would not be made any more certain with proof – if proof were possible. There is no need to prove that the world and other people exist, just as there is no need to prove that tables can't sing arias or that carafes cannot at the same time be women. Stated, put into language, they are self-evident truths, which cannot and need not be proved. They are among the truths required for there to be proof of anything else – truths without which there is no understanding.

Descartes thought he could begin with no self-evident truths beyond the solipsistic *Cogito, ergo sum.* He thereby set a pattern in philosophy: Western philosophers since then have tried to "start at zero and build a system," as Frithjof Schuon, the great scholar of the world's religions, summed it up with astute common-sense simplicity. But of course you cannot start at zero. At zero, thinking would not be possible.

Thomas Reid made this point in one of the most delightful and commonsensical passages in all of Western philosophy:

A man that disbelieves his own existence, is surely as unfit to be reasoned with as a man that believes he is made of glass. There may be disorders in the human frame that may produce such extravagancies, but they will never be cured by reasoning. Des Cartes, indeed, would make us believe he got out of this delirium by this logical argument, "Cogito, ergo, sum"; but it is evident he was in his senses all the time, and never seriously doubted of his existence; for he takes it for granted in this argument, and proves nothing at all.

Descartes did not start anywhere near zero. By bringing in language, as he necessarily did in conducting his philosophical inquiry, he brought in the world of common sense and common experience that language is rooted in. Thus he illustrated Reid's maxim that philosophy "has no other root but the principles of Common Sense; it grows out of them, and draws its nourishment from them."

B ELOW COMMON SENSE, the philosopher as philosopher cannot go. The human being can, and does – in dreams, delirium, dementia, dreamless sleep, or unconsciousness. But where we actually take our stand in life, and in our thinking, is in the realm of our shared experience, the language we speak in common with others, and the common-sense truths of our experience. To be a thinking human being is to be a person among other people in the common-sense world.

If you pause to consider all this, you will realize that common sense is the foundation of all we know, the foundation of the very possibility of knowing anything.

Even the most sophisticated theoretical knowledge rests on a foundation of common sense. This is true in two different ways. A brilliant Nobel Prize–winning physicist at Berkeley must rely on his common sense to get dressed in the morning, make his coffee, eat breakfast, then drive safely to campus. His ability to conduct his research depends on his ability to operate in the world of common sense he shares with all of us. But common sense is also the foundation of knowing on a deeper level: it is the foundation of human understanding in all its aspects. Leo Strauss made this point very elegantly in *Natural Right and History*:

[T]here is an articulation of reality that precedes all scientific articulation: that articulation, that wealth of meaning, which we have in mind when speaking of the world of common experience or of the natural understanding of the world.... Since the natural understanding is the presupposition of the scientific understanding, the analysis of science and the world of science presupposes the analysis of the natural understanding, the natural world, or the world of common sense.

This is true of science and of every other branch of human understanding. Common sense is quite simply the basis of all human knowledge, even the most advanced knowledge. It is the basis of the very possibility of knowledge.

Science depends on common sense. This means that there are common-sense truths without which science is impossible. It follows that there are common-sense truths with a higher degree of certainty than science can supply.

DOING SCIENCE

Any physical theory is always provisional, in the sense that it is only a hypothesis: you can never prove it. No matter how many times the results of experiments agree with some theory, you can never be sure that the next time the result will not contradict the theory.

STEPHEN HAWKING
A Brief History of Time

You hear people speaking of "scientific proof," don't you? That phrase is used only by people who do not understand science. When someone – even a scientist! – tells you that science has proved something, you can be certain that "science" has not done so. Gregory Bateson makes the point emphatically in *Mind and Nature* (with capitals and italics): "SCIENCE NEVER PROVES ANYTHING. Science sometimes *improves* hypotheses and sometimes *disproves* them. But *proof* would be another matter." He then puts it concisely: "Science *probes*; it does not prove."

While mathematics and logic work by proofs, scientists don't deal in proofs. "The work of the scientist consists in putting forward and testing theories," as the philosopher Karl Popper explained. Scientists test theories with experiments. All scientific theories are provisional, and may be contradicted by new evidence at any time. That is the significance of the word "theory."

Newton's theory of gravitational motion once defined an epoch. Newton unified the preceding theories of Galileo and of Kepler by correcting them and also explaining them on a higher level of universality. This was an awesome achievement. For over two centuries, its explanatory powers made it seem invincible. But it was eventually superseded by Einstein's theory of relativity. There are scientists right now working on problems in physics generated by Einstein's awesome theory. As robust and well-tested as it is, no doubt some new theory will someday do to Einstein's theory what Einstein's theory did to Newton's.

Both Newton's and Einstein's theories are testable. A scientific theory must necessarily be stated in such a way as to be testable, and there must be a possibility of demonstrating that it is erroneous. In other words, it must be falsifiable.

Einstein was perfectly clear about this. He insisted that his equations had to be tested experimentally, and he offered three tests for this purpose. The most famous concerned his prediction of precisely how much a ray of light would be bent by passing close to the sun during a solar eclipse. He said it would be 1.745 seconds of arc. But a verification of that prediction was not enough for Einstein. He insisted that all three tests needed to be met. Concerning the third experiment, he wrote: "If it were proved that this effect does not exist in nature, then the whole theory would have to be abandoned." Keep in mind that those experiments could not prove the theory to be true; they could only provide corroboration by eliminating specific ways it might be in error.

Although Einstein in no way suggested that "truth is relative," his place in the history of science illustrates the provisional nature of scientific findings. Karl Popper elaborates on this point:

Scientific results are "relative" (if this term is to be used at all) only in so far as they are the results of a certain stage of scientific development and liable to be superseded in the course of scientific progress. But this does not mean that truth is "relative". If an assertion is true, it is true forever. It only means that most scientific results have the character of hypotheses, i.e. statements ... which are ... liable to revision at any time.

A scientific theory, again, must be falsifiable. By contrast, the statement that carafes cannot also at the same time be women is not falsifiable. It is not a theory. It is a truth of common sense.

"But wait," you might say. "Wasn't it once common sense that the sun revolves around the earth?" Well, no. The belief that the sun revolves around the earth was only a theory, though it was widely held for obvious reasons. It was based on certain credible observations, and it was overthrown by superior observations. A medieval ploughman could know it was time for his midday meal by observing the position of the sun in the sky, and today we can still rely on the same annual patterns of "sunrise" and "sunset" that structured his days. But someone who told the ploughman that the sun rose to its noonday height and descended to the horizon again by orbiting the earth would be presenting a *theoretical* account – an idea that was testable.

Is where we have arrived surprising to you? Common-sense truths that have more certainty than science! This is not in line with the way people generally view science and common sense.

Those who are dismissive of common sense are thinking of it merely as the collective opinions of the crowd, but that is not what common sense is. Let's turn again to *Roget's Thesaurus* for help here. These are the entries for common sense: "good sense, savvy, sound judgment, native intelligence, horse sense, prudence, acumen, level-headedness, instinct, wisdom, experience." *Roget's* also quotes Ralph Waldo Emerson: "Genius dressed in its working clothes." What we are getting at when we speak of common sense is a power of knowing. And we have seen that common sense enables us to know a vast array of truths. It even tells us truths that cannot be challenged without undermining the very possibility of reasoning or understanding.

There is a well-known story, one you have probably heard, that illustrates the relationship between common sense and science. The story has circulated in several versions, one of them featuring the American philosopher William James.

After giving a public lecture on the structure of the solar system, James was approached by a little old lady who challenged his presentation:

"Your theory that the sun is the center of the solar

system and the earth is a ball which rotates around it has a very convincing ring to it, Mr. James, but it's wrong," she said. "I've got a better theory."

"And what is that?" James inquired politely.

"That we live on a crust of earth which is on the back of a giant turtle."

"If your theory is correct," James asked, "what does this turtle stand on?"

"You're a very clever man, Mr. James, and that's a very good question," replied the little old lady, "but I have an answer to it. And it is this: The first turtle stands on the back of a second, far larger turtle, which stands directly under him."

"But what does this second turtle stand on?"

"It's no use, Mr. James – it's turtles all the way down."

There is a lot going on here. We have a philosopher giving a public lecture on how the solar system works. So, we have science and philosophy. We also have the human need to understand our world, which gives rise to science and philosophy, and which filled the hall with people interested in learning about the solar system. And there is the lady's bizarre challenge to the model of the solar system that James presented.

Of course, that scientific model was subject to challenge. In fact, it has since been revised, as the outer boundary of the solar system was expanded to include the planet Pluto. Today, Pluto is still there but it is no longer a planet. What's more, astronomers now say that at least 90 percent of the solar system is beyond the orbit of Pluto. No doubt our picture of the solar system will continue to change as long as astronomers keep acquiring better and more powerful tools to study our neighborhood of the Milky Way.

But the little old lady was not offering the kind of challenge that brought these advances in our understanding of the solar system, and James understood that an argument from science was not going to work with her. An expert presentation of the latest findings in astronomy would have been useless. Instead, he made his appeal to common sense. Leaving aside whether the turtles were scientifically plausible, he focused on the fact that her response didn't answer the question, since it had no end point.

Explanations must finally have a stopping point. Whenever it is shown that an explanation involves an infinite regress, the explanation has failed. That's just common sense. When the little old lady rejected the appeal to common sense, the discussion came to an impasse.

What makes the story so fascinating is that it is a perfect example of how a sudden change in the context is often what makes a joke funny. The story begins with James discussing the world *on* which we live. When the little old lady introduces her theory, it becomes a story about the common-sense world *in* which we live as persons among other people. In that world, we operate by common sense.

DOING PSYCHOTHERAPY

The psychoanalyst aims at establishing rational,
voluntary self-control ....

HERBERT FINGARETTE
The Self in Transformation: Psychoanalysis,
Philosophy and the Life of the Spirit

THE LITTLE OLD LADY who told William James her
theory of "turtles all the way down" may not have
required psychotherapy, if her whimsical notions did
not interfere with navigating the everyday world. But
some people struggle to find a way into a life grounded
in ordinary common sense. That is the subject matter
of psychotherapy, though it is not generally thought or
spoken of in those terms. If you pause for a moment to
consider any familiar example of therapy, however, you
will realize that the goal in every case is to anchor the
patient in the common-sense world we share.

For instance, if you are acquainted with the history
of psychoanalysis, you will have heard of the famous case
of Little Hans. It is one of Freud's best-known early
cases, and it helped him define the field of psychoanalysis. Hans was a boy with a phobia of horses. The whole
point of treatment was to relieve him of his phobia so

he could live with horses as other people were able to do in a society that depended on horses for transportation. To put it another way, the goal of treatment was to enable Hans to live with the ordinary common-sense truths about living with horses – truths about the risks *and* the safety.

Little Hans suffered from a pattern of feelings and behavior at odds with ordinary human understanding and action. Therapy would be successful to the extent that Hans joined others in a world where boys are eager to learn to ride horses instead of being afflicted by a morbid fear of horses.

Stated in the language of common sense, the purpose of the therapist's skills and the therapeutic relationship is to help the patient overcome a dysfunctional pattern of feelings and behavior, and be able to join the realm of common sense and shared experience. The therapist's task is to understand the problem in the patient's own terms – in essence, to enter the patient's private world of affliction – in order to help find a way out of the impasse that led to the search for help.

From time to time, a therapist may be successful by making a direct appeal to common sense, instead of relying on orthodox therapeutic techniques. Dr. Irvin Yalom, a psychiatrist and professor of psychiatry at Stanford, offers a particularly striking and unusual illustration of using common sense as a therapeutic tool in his book *Love's Executioner and Other Tales of Psychiatry.*

Yalom writes about a patient he calls Carlos, who

"had always prowled for women and regarded them in highly sexualized and demeaning terms." Carlos's sexualized attitude toward two women in his therapy group precipitated a crisis, requiring Yalom's intervention. Carlos tells Yalom "what I want to do with those two [here he uses explicit and vulgar language]. I meant it when I said that if rape were legal, I'd do it! And I know just where I would start!"

Here is the exchange that followed, as Yalom records:

"All right, Carlos, let's consider this ideal society you're imagining and advocating – this society of legalized rape. Think now, for a few minutes, about your daughter. How would it be for her living in the community – being available for legal rape …?"

Suddenly Carlos stopped grinning. He winced visibly and said simply, "I wouldn't like that for her."

"… what do you really want for her?"

"I want her to have a loving relationship with a man and have a loving family."

"But how can that happen if her father is advocating a world of rape?"

That Yalom is using an appeal to common sense could not be more obvious. We have not traveled so very far from P. J. O'Rourke's appeal to common sense. A world of teenage boys armed with whiskey and cars, and a world of legal rape: both scenarios depart from the standards of our common-sense world in ways that are not dissimilar.

Such a direct appeal to common sense is hardly standard in psychotherapy. On the contrary, it is more often the powerful technique of the grandmother, not the psychiatrist. In fact, Yalom writes that "the tactic seemed so contrived and so simplistic that I could not possibly have predicted the astonishing result it would produce." Yet it did work in the case of Carlos.

Whether the therapist uses a nonstandard appeal to common sense or the standard techniques in which the therapist meets the patient where the patient's trouble is while staying anchored in the world of common sense, the whole point of the enterprise is for the patient eventually to meet the therapist on the shared ground of common sense.

THE RECOVERY OF A more severely ill psychiatric patient is also recognizably a return to the world of common sense. Years ago I treated a patient who provided a vivid illustration of this point.

During her initial consultation, she was arguing loudly (you could hear her from a long way off) with two other people, a man and a woman. The problem was that no one else could see the other man or the other woman. She shouted at them, turning her head from one to the other, demanding that the man stop interrupting her, telling the woman that she was a liar, and so on. It was fascinating. I felt I could almost follow the course of the argument, despite the fact that I was only hearing one side of a three-sided fight. I thought at the time that it could have been the inspiration for an interesting one-act play. Her husband told me she had been this way for several years, as I recall.

On her second consultation, she was still shouting just as loudly as before. But there was a difference. This time she was shouting at her husband. He looked at me with an aggrieved expression and asked me pointedly, "This is better?" I replied that she had made progress under treatment, since we knew that the person being shouted at was actually present.

The next time, I was the target of her shouting. Her husband asked me how I liked it, but this too was progress. She was dealing with a real person, and one whom she had less reason to trust than her husband. Since I was interfering with her life, the accusations she hurled at me had a real function in the common-sense world. She was still a deeply disturbed person, but she had gained a toehold on the common-sense world in which we all meet.

It is remarkable how well the language of common sense functions in the realm of psychotherapy, isn't it? That is so because it is a powerful and supple language for understanding the self, and the self among other selves. It is the natural language of our efforts for personal growth, in psychotherapy and in more ordinary circumstances too.

GAINING SELF-MASTERY

"A few years will settle her opinions on the reasonable basis
of common sense and observation."

JANE AUSTEN
Sense and Sensibility

WHAT DIFFERENCE DOES a few years make? Let's
return for a moment to P. J. O'Rourke's comment about
giving whiskey and car keys to teenage boys, and then
imagine this scenario: A well-groomed middle-aged man
exits a liquor store and walks toward his car. He holds
a shopping bag containing a bottle of whiskey in one
hand, and his car keys in the other. This does not cause
you any concern. Why not?

If you are not alarmed it is because you assume that
the middle-aged man is a grown-up. But what does that
actually mean? A grown-up is someone who has achieved
a certain basic level of common sense. This means that
the process of growing up is a process of acquiring common sense. The teenager is further along in that process
than the small child who is not yet advanced enough to
be trusted to handle sharp knives, and the teenager is
not yet as far along as the mature adult who can be
trusted with whiskey and car keys.

Since acquiring common sense is a process, it follows that common sense is something that can be developed. We often learn best from stories, so we'll turn to Jane Austen for an illustration of how this might happen.

Austen's brilliant novel *Sense and Sensibility* (and Ang Lee's captivating 1995 film starring Emma Thompson and Kate Winslet) can teach us quite a lot about common sense. It is the story of two sisters: Elinor loves a man who is committed to another woman, while Marianne is in love with a scoundrel. The title announces the novel's double theme, and each theme is exemplified by one of the central characters.

The title conveyed a clear and precise meaning to readers in Austen's time, which is easily missed today. "Sense" is the easier of the two for us to understand: it meant "common sense." Translating the title so that it reads "Common Sense and Sensibility" gets us going in the right direction about the first of the two words. It does not take us all the way, however, for the simple reason that Austen and her readers had a much more robust conception of common sense than we do today.

Our challenge in understanding what Austen meant by sensibility is greater. As a result of many changes in our attitudes and our speech, many of us will miss Austen's meaning. To understand it, let's consider the root word, "sensible." We still use it, but usually in a very different way than it is used in the novel and was in Austen's day generally. If we commend someone for making a sensible decision, we might also say that the decision showed common sense. But when Marianne, defending her own conduct, tells Elinor, "I am not sensible of having done anything wrong in walking over Mrs. Smith's grounds," she means that she has no feeling of having done anything wrong. In Austen's day, sensibility meant a capacity for emotional responses to one's experiences. Persons of strong sensibility could be counted on to display and express the feelings aroused in them by poetry, music, and picturesque scenery. They would also be inclined to display and express the emotions aroused in them by life's ups and downs, as Marianne's story illustrates.

At the time, both common sense and sensibility were considered to be fundamental human faculties, possessed by all of us. Each could be cultivated and developed, or neglected and therefore stunted. To a large extent, this was the explanation of the readily observable fact that people have more or less common sense, and differ widely in how emotionally expressive they are.

So, to understand the novel on a level deeper than the narrative of events, we need to see that Elinor and Marianne personify these two fundamentals of human nature. Elinor represents common sense. Marianne embodies sensibility and the romantic impulse to put emotion first in one's life. Near the beginning of the novel, Austen establishes the contrast when Elinor says that her sister's "opinions are all romantic," but then goes on to predict, "A few years will settle her opinions on the reasonable basis of common sense and observation."

Austen first shows us the romantic sensibility at work, as Marianne rashly gives her love to an unprincipled rogue. When he jilts her, she embraces the martyrdom of love with equal rashness:

Marianne would have thought herself very inexcusable had she been able to sleep at all the first night after parting with Willoughby. She would have been ashamed to look her family in the face the next morning, had she not risen from her bed in more need of repose than when she lay down in it.... She was awake the whole night, and she wept the greatest part of it. She got up with a headache, was unable to talk, and unwilling to take any nourishment; giving pain every moment to her mother and sisters, and forbidding all attempt at consolation from either. Her sensibility was potent enough!...

The evening passed off in the equal indulgence of feeling.... and this nourishment of grief was every day applied.

Austen draws the contrast with Elinor very clearly. When she in her turn is disappointed in love, instead of yielding to her feelings, Elinor shows "her determination to subdue" them. Austen writes repeatedly of Elinor's "self-command." Marianne, however, is not impressed by it:

Such behavior as this, so exactly the reverse of her own, appeared no more meritorious to Marianne, than her own had seemed faulty to her. The business of self-command she settled very easily; – with strong affections it was impossible, with calm ones it could have no merit.

From Marianne's standpoint, Elinor's conduct can only mean that she does not love deeply, but we know better. It is not by chance that the scene near the end of the story in which Elinor and her beloved are finally united is one of the most deeply emotional moments in all of Austen's novels and is the most moving scene in the film.

Marianne's self-indulgence eventually results in a life-threatening illness. Elinor puts aside her own grief to nurse her sister, and eventually helps bring her around to a change of perspective.

Marianne says of her own conduct, "I compare it with what it ought to have been; I compare it with yours."

Elinor responds, "Our situations have borne little resemblance." Then Marianne explains what she has learned:

"My illness has made me think.... I considered the past: I saw in my own behavior ... nothing but a series of imprudence towards myself, and want of kindness to others. I saw that my own feelings had prepared my sufferings, and that my want of fortitude under them had almost led me to the grave. My illness, I well knew, had been entirely brought on by myself, by such negligence of my own health as I felt even at the time to be wrong. Had I died, it would have been self-destruction."

This is the fulfillment of Elinor's prophecy that Marianne will in time gain a reasonable, common-sense perspective on her situation. We are left in no doubt where Austen comes down on the issue of common sense and sensibility. Bringing the two into a proper balance is the way to self-mastery.

Oᴜʀ ᴇxᴀᴍɪɴᴀᴛɪᴏɴ ᴏꜰ common sense and sensibility in Jane Austen's world gives us another lens through which to view Stiva's dream in *Anna Karenina*. Earlier we focused on how Tolstoy portrayed the absence of common-sense principles in the dream world; now let's read the passage again with an eye to sensibility (emphasis added):

Stiva ... opened his eyes. "Yes, yes, how did it go?" he thought, recalling his dream. "Yes! Alabin was giving a dinner in Darmstadt – no, not in Darmstadt but something American. Yes, but this Darmstadt was in America. Yes, Alabin was giving a dinner on glass tables, yes – and the tables were singing Il mio Tesoro, *only it wasn't* Il mio Tesoro *but something better, and there were some little carafes, which were also women," he recalled.* His eyes glittered merrily, and he fell to thinking with a smile. "Yes, it was nice, very nice. *There were many other excellent things there, but one can't say it in words, or even put it into waking thoughts."*

The dream world, Tolstoy shows us, is a world of heightened sensibility. From delight-filled dreams like Stiva's to terrifying nightmares, emotional intensity is the hallmark of the dream. The content of Stiva's dream may be somewhat confusing and difficult for him to convey, but Stiva's delight in his dream, his emotional response to his dream, comes through with perfect clarity. In our dreams, the absence of common sense brings sensibility to the fore.

We know this from our own experience. Our emotional responses to our dreams are paramount, and we commonly categorize our dreams on that basis. In the turbulent world of dreams there are nightmares, anxiety dreams, sweet dreams, dreams filled with violent emotions, nostalgic dreams, dreams filled with a feeling of dread, and so on through the whole gamut of feelings.

In our waking life, a lack of common sense brings sensibility to the fore. Austen shows us that Marianne's choice to elevate sensibility over common sense gave her life a turbulent and dreamlike quality. As we are likely to say in telling her story, her sweet dreams of perfect romance gave way to nightmares of rejection and humiliation, of longing and nostalgia, of despair.

Let's take another look at Marianne's reflection on the danger she had put herself in. We may miss something about it that readers in Austen's day were likely to recognize. Marianne here runs down the list of the cardinal, or principal, virtues in terms of their opposites: prudence ("imprudence"), fortitude ("want of fortitude"), justice ("want of kindness to others"), and temperance (the dangerous intemperance of her behavior overall). The cardinal virtues were also called the natural virtues, and each was understood to be like one of the four cardinal directions on a compass.

They might also be called the common-sense virtues. Prudence and temperance are so closely allied with common sense that there is little need to argue the point, and it is also easy to link fortitude and justice to common sense. Urging Marianne to be strong or to consider the feelings of others might have been the appropriate common-sense advice at various points in her ordeal.

The point, which would not have been lost on readers in Austen's day, is that common sense gives us more than the ability to make prudent and practical choices that are likely to have good outcomes. Common sense, it was held, gives us the ability to make choices that are right in moral terms as well. For Austen and her readers at the time, prudence was more than the practical ability to size up a situation and make a choice that works for us; it was a virtue, and a necessary one.

In the heightened sensibility of the dream state, the rules of morality and decorum are lost along with the principles of common sense. We do things in our dreams that we would never do in our waking lives. The bad passions and troublesome impulses within each of us are only too ready to come out and have in our dreams that holiday we try to deny them in our waking lives. If we all behaved today as we dreamed we behaved last night, what an astonishing day it would be!

The idea that common sense encompasses the virtues or that prudence itself is a virtue is very far from the way we tend to think about common sense today. Yet Austen has shown us that common sense and prudence enable a person to make decisions and judgments that are sound both practically and morally. It is interesting to note that Thomas Reid, the father of the philosophy of common-sense realism, included the human capacity to make judgments about what is morally right in his account of common sense. In the dedication of his *Inquiry into the Human Mind on the Principles of Common Sense*, he presented himself as being motivated by a moral concern to defend "piety, patriotism, friendship, parental affection and private virtue."

C. S. Lewis, in commenting on *Sense and Sensibility*, wrote of "the grammar of conduct." His point was that grammar is something that anyone can learn, and that everyone must learn in order to master the use of language and enjoy its benefits. In the same way, mastering the grammar of conduct enables us to maximize the benefits to be gained by applying the principles of common sense in the conduct of our lives. It is a key to self-mastery.

SELF–MASTERY AND
SELF–RULE

The same degree of understanding which makes a man
capable of acting with common prudence in the conduct of
life makes him capable of discovering what is true and
what is false in matters that are self-evident . . . .

THOMAS REID
Essays on the Intellectual Powers of Man

ACCORDING TO Thomas Reid, the test of common
sense is the ability to act with prudence in the conduct
of life. Jane Austen agreed. They were contemporaries:
he lived from 1710 to 1796; she lived from 1775 to 1817.
During Austen's lifetime, Reid was influential in both
Great Britain and America. Reid offers incisive philosophy for the philosophically minded among us, while
Austen, in *Sense and Sensibility*, offers a captivating por-
trayal of that philosophy in story form for the rest of us.

For Reid, the path to knowledge is "the way of observation." Austen could hardly have been more explicit in
making the same point when Elinor says that Marianne
in time will "settle her opinions on the reasonable basis
of common sense and observation." Austen's story of
Elinor and Marianne portrays the important truth that

as we gain in common sense we move along the path of self-mastery.

The American Founders applied the same idea to politics – and they drew a world-changing conclusion. Their wild and crazy notion was that people who are capable of *personal* self-rule by common sense are also capable of *political* self-rule by common sense. A philosophy of common sense, with its respect for people of common sense, is what makes America's robust conception of the citizen possible. In the Founders' vision, the ultimate foundation of American self-rule is the common sense of the American people. The Founders staked their lives, their fortunes, and their sacred honor on their belief that the American people were capable of self-rule. (By the way, this is what the book *Common Sense Nation* is all about.)

THE AMERICANS of the founding generation declared that all people are created equal. They did not stop there. They also claimed that the equality of persons is "self-evident." They did not claim that it is a political or social theory. Their claim was that it is one of the self-evident truths of common sense.

Reid spoke of discovering what is true and false in matters that are self-evident. This means that while some self-evident truths are readily apparent to the person of common sense, other self-evident truths must be found. Self-evident does not mean obvious. The truth that a carafe cannot at the same time be a woman – like countless instances of that principle of identity (a woman cannot at the same time be a hat, and so on) – is readily apparent. But the truth that all people are created equal was not readily apparent in a world with hereditary monarchies and hereditary ruling classes. This truth had to be discovered. The claim of common-sense thinkers is that once it was understood, it was self-evidently true.

To grasp this idea of discovering a truth that is self-evident, let's start with an example from arithmetic: $2 + 2 = 4$. To know this is true, we need to have learned the meaning of the figures and symbols, and perhaps have seen the equation demonstrated graphically when we were children. It was true before we learned the terms and concepts, but we need that basic understanding before we can recognize the truth. Henceforward we are likely to be certain of its truth. A self-evident truth is known to be true by everyone who grasps the meaning of the terms used to express it. No proof is required, though a process of discovery may be necessary.

How then do we go about discovering the self-evident truth that "all men are created equal"? We start with this: It is self-evident that no person is *by nature* the ruler of other people in the way that people are by nature the rulers of horses and cattle. "The subjection of the horse to the rider is according to nature," writes Harry Jaffa in his truly great book *A New Birth of Freedom.* By contrast, "Nature has made no such distinction between man and man."

Thomas Jefferson described this as a "palpable truth" that was being discovered by more and more people:

All eyes are open to or opening to ... the palpable truth that the mass of mankind has not been born with saddles on their backs, nor a favored few booted and spurred, ready to ride them legitimately, by the grace of God.

When we find a situation in which some men rule over others, it arises from a human arrangement or convention, as Jaffa notes in commenting on Jefferson's statement:

The queen bee is marked out by nature for her function in the hive. Human queens (or kings) are not so marked. Their rule is conventional, not natural. As we have seen Jefferson say, human beings are not born with saddles on their backs, and others booted and spurred to ride them. These are facts accessible to everyone. They are truths that are self-evident.

So it is not just true, but self-evidently true that no human being is born to rule over other human beings.

If WE CAN KNOW self-evident truths by common sense, and if we can discover truths that are self-evident, this means that what is known by common sense evolves over time.

The idea that humanity advances by an evolutionary growth in knowledge and knowhow was articulated by Adam Ferguson, who became Professor of Moral Philosophy at the University of Edinburgh in 1764, the same year that Thomas Reid was appointed Professor of Moral Philosophy at the University of Glasgow. In his delightful and very readable book *An Essay on the*

History of Civil Society, published in 1767, Ferguson wrote that we move forward in a largely unplanned way:

Mankind, in following the present sense of their minds, in striving to remove inconveniences, or to gain apparent and contiguous advantages, arrive at ends which even their imagination could not anticipate; and pass on ... without perceiving its end. He who first said, "I will appropriate this field; I will leave it to my heirs;" did not perceive, that he was laying the foundation of civil laws and political establishments....

Every step and every movement of the multitude, even in what are termed enlightened ages, are made with equal blindness to the future; and nations stumble on establishments, which are indeed the result of human action, but not the execution of any human design.

Ferguson's great insight was that human progress occurs by an evolutionary process of trial and error more than by design. In essence, experiments are conducted by many people, dispersed over space and time, in their everyday lives, and knowledge is accumulated as a result.

The great human achievement of language emerged in this way. It was "made by humankind, but not planned," as Matt Ridley points out. "There is no government, supreme court or police force of the English language yet we all obey its laws of vocabulary, grammar, and syntax." The language we speak is filled with wisdom born of vast, cumulative experience of human life. For one simple example, we speak of things that are *good* – a good horse, a good person, a good deed. No authority or committee decided the meaning of *good*. The word and the concept emerged out of our shared experience, and the meaning was reinforced by repetition. Likewise, our law and institutions, morals and customs embody the experience of many generations. They have stood the test of time, and they are gifts of common sense.

The principle of evolutionary growth applies even in a rapidly advancing society like ours. When someone comes up with a better way of doing something, it is quickly adopted by others and becomes simply the way we do things. There is no general plan that we all change our habits. Rather, we see what works by observation and common sense. Our society welcomes innovation to a degree that would astonish people who lived in times when the human world was about the same for the grandson as it had been for the grandfather. But no central authority designed either that society or the one in which we live – as Adam Ferguson brilliantly observed.

Ferguson's powerful insight points us toward many fascinating topics. For example, it explains why attempts at central planning of societies and economies always fail – are in fact doomed to failure. Ferguson's idea of *social evolution* by trial and error, as people learn from each other, suggested to Darwin and others the theory of *biological evolution* by natural selection from spontaneous trial and error in nature.

For our purposes, the important point is that Ferguson showed how the substance of common-sense knowledge evolves. The fundamental principles of common sense are unchanging, but our common understanding of the world has changed over the ages. As that understanding evolves, so does the world of human action.

We make our way forward in an unplanned, shared process of learning by common sense, our fundamental mode of knowing, as well as by the special, professionalized mode of learning that we call science.

America was founded on respect for common sense and ordinary prudence, but "sophisticated" Americans have long discounted their importance for understanding our world and acting within it. They have led an attack on common sense in the service of a radical political agenda, one that is antithetical to the Founders' vision and to the wisdom of ordinary Americans, as we shall see.

REJECTING COMMON SENSE

Philosophical thought begins with the recognition that the facts do not correspond to the concepts imposed by common sense and scientific reason – in short, with the refusal to accept them.

HERBERT MARCUSE
"A Note on Dialectics"

HERBERT MARCUSE (1898–1979) was trained in philosophy in his native Germany, but he came to America in 1934 and here enjoyed great celebrity. When I was a university student in the 1960s, Marcuse was all the rage on campus. The dictum of the New Left was: *Marx is the prophet, Marcuse is his interpreter, and Mao is the sword.*

Fashions have changed, and college students no longer hold aloft Mao's *Little Red Book* as they march in their demonstrations. But the influence of Marcuse lives on. "The struggle against common sense is the beginning of speculative thinking," Marcuse declared. Today the struggle against common sense and the refusal to accept what it shows us have permeated thinking – and not just speculative thinking – on the political left.

What could be the reason for rejecting common

sense? From the leftist perspective, the problem with common sense is that it led to the wrong revolution – the American Revolution. Even worse, the American Revolution was a success. The American republic provided its citizens with liberty and opportunity far beyond anything that human beings had ever known before.

In contrast, the revolutions based on Marxist thinking failed, and failed spectacularly. The Soviet Union murdered its own people in the tens of millions and then collapsed, in part as the result of attempting the impossible: trying to run a country according to Marxist economic ideas. The rulers of countries like Cuba or North Korea who continue to declare their allegiance to Marxist doctrines keep themselves in power by force and run their countries for their own benefit.

The lesson of history is clear, yet the Left refuses to accept it. This remarkable fact requires some kind of explanation.

To understand this strange state of affairs, we must acknowledge that many people found Marx's ideas appealing. Whatever else is true about those ideas, they inspired vast numbers of people. Those numbers and the intensity of that inspiration changed the course of history. All this is undeniable.

What the believers in Marxist doctrines deny is that the failure of those ideas to work wherever they have been tried must mean that the ideas are wrong.

Marx claimed that he had founded a science. Because he believed it was a science, he believed it enabled him to make predictions about the future. But his predictions did not come about. In addition, the many attempts by various countries to set up systems applying his "science" have not worked as he claimed they would. In fact, they have not worked at all well. In scientific terms, it is clear that those Marxist experiments have "falsified" the Marxist doctrines. In terms of common sense, the misery of those who have suffered poverty and oppression under Marxist systems tells us all we need to know to conclude that Marxism has failed.

However, Marxists did not want to accept that outcome. Instead of acknowledging the clear verdict of history and common sense, they stuck with their ideology. They were unwilling to accept that a verdict had even been reached. Amazingly, they decided that they faced not a verdict but a choice: Marxism or rationality. So great was their attachment to Marxism that they chose to abandon rationality. Marxism had failed as science – so then, out with science! Marxism had failed the tests of common sense – so then, out with common sense! Hence Marcuse's "refusal to accept" either common sense or scientific reason. Better to abandon rationality than to accept that Marxism failed.

Common-sense thinking and common-sense philosophy are all about understanding the reality of ourselves and our circumstances. A common-sense understanding of the world resulted in a philosophical and political revolution: the American Revolution. That revolution challenged the legitimacy of the political order that predominated at the time – the order in which the absolutism of monarchs was backed by an official religion. Today, only primitive and backward countries like Saudi Arabia still have such systems.

The American Revolution succeeded and its influence spread because it was rooted in common sense. By contrast, leftist political revolutions defied common sense, and their failure led to an open rejection of common sense.

Everyone knows, or rather everyone ought to know, that government is always and everywhere inefficient. It's a common-sense observation, based on the normal experience of government. Yet for the Left, government is always and everywhere the solution.

I was fortunate to get an early lesson in how government works when I was employed by the federal government one summer. It taught me a common-sense truth or two about government and preserved me from the worst follies of Marxist thinking.

The federal government, in its restless search for problems to solve, discovered in the early 1960s that many college students wanted summer jobs. This fact was declared to be a "problem" (or perhaps it was called a "crisis"; I don't recall). The plan devised for solving the problem was – surprise! – to throw money at it. Federal bureaucrats were given more money and power (which, as P. J. O'Rourke said, is dangerous) in order to provide summer jobs for college students.

I got a position at the motor pool on a military base. And a position is literally what it was. It was the middle position on the bench seat of a truck. My job was to occupy that part of the seat. I spent eight hours, five days a week, sitting between the driver and his assistant. The government had decreed "let there be jobs" and – lo and behold! – jobs appeared. But there was nothing for me to do, except to coordinate with the driver so as not to interfere with his operation of the floor shift.

For that matter, there was almost no work for the other two men in that truck. The civil service commissar who ruled the motor pool had two rules: 1) Always look busy. 2) Constantly vary where you eat lunch. Occasionally he did assign us tasks. Now and then we made deliveries, usually transferring furniture from one place to another. But mostly our days consisted of racing around the navy base as if we were on urgent business, while keeping an eye out for pleasant spots to open our lunch boxes and enjoy not being in the truck. That was it.

The driver and his copilot were pleasant fellows who took a friendly interest in me. The navy base covered a vast area of great natural beauty, and my colleagues kindly made sure that I got to experience all the best spots. And the money was great – much better than any summer job in the private sector. In fact, more than fourteen years were to pass before I made as much money again. Because I was living at my parents' home, I was able to save nearly everything after taxes, so my college fund grew rapidly. All in all, you would think this was a very good deal for a college kid who needed money to get through the school year. Nonetheless, I could take it only for so long. I quit about halfway through the summer.

Whether or not it was a good deal for me, it was not such a good deal for the taxpayers.

The lesson about the problem with government is perfectly clear: the incentives are upside down. To see the point, think about how a similar operation would work in the private sector, where the laws of economics cannot be ignored. Imagine that the commissar had been the owner of a trucking business instead of being the administrator of a government operation. He would have had to raise money, and quite a lot of it, to go into that business in the first place – not just requisition it from taxpayers. In order to stay in business, he would have had to make a profit. That means he would have had to keep us busy doing something that brought in enough value to pay our salaries and his other costs, with profit on top, instead of simply telling us to look busy.

Because our boss was a government administrator instead of a businessman, it meant that the more money he spent and the more trucks in the motor pool and the more people reporting to him, the better for his career – regardless of what was accomplished with it all. Those bigger numbers were the basis for determining his civil service rank, and therefore his pay and benefits. He had no incentive to provide value for the taxpayers who were funding the effort.

Here we have in a nutshell the explanation for what we keep learning about government programs. For one example, there is the terrible scandal at the Veterans Health Administration that briefly got the public's attention not long ago. The problem was that VA doctors had no incentive to help the veterans, as they were safe from being fired, while the veterans were essentially trapped in the system, with little ability to shop for better service. The scandalous conditions at VA hospitals and clinics were entirely predictable, and in fact could have been predicted when the system was set up – just as similarly scandalous conditions will be entirely predictable if and when the Left manages to achieve its dream of government-controlled health care for everyone in America, so that we are all trapped in the system.

It's common sense that a government program to give summer jobs to college students will result only in a temporary increase in the number of government workers with not enough to do. Likewise, it's common sense that government spending to stimulate the economy is going to enrich interest groups and people favored by those in government who hand out the money, and that the inevitable waste involved will actually harm the economy. Since governmental folly and corruption is a story as old as the hills, plain common sense could have spared our military veterans from the horrors at the VA and ought to spare us all from what awaits if the federal government takes over our health care.

But Americans no longer seem to be able to mount political arguments that are confidently grounded in common sense – or that prevail in the public forum if they are presented. Because arguments from common sense have lost the power they once had in American public discourse, our future may actually include such follies as a takeover of health care by the federal government.

How did this come about? To find the answer, we must go back to the time of the American founding, and to another place.

ROMANTICISM

*It seems to me to be the greatest single shift in the con-
sciousness of the West that has occurred, and all the other
shifts which have occurred in the course of the nineteenth
and twentieth centuries appear to me in comparison less
important, and at any rate deeply influenced by it.*

ISAIAH BERLIN
The Roots of Romanticism

ISAIAH BERLIN identified a transformation of the
European consciousness without parallel in the years
between 1760 and 1830, when the era of the Enlightenment was giving way to the era of romanticism. The
romantics, he wrote, discarded "the tradition that there
is a nature of things which must be learnt, which must
be understood, which must be known, and to which
people must adjust themselves." They rebelled against
the traditional understanding that there is an objective
pattern to the world and the cosmos. That tradition, as
C. S. Lewis observed in *A Preface to Paradise Lost*, was
"never, in essence, assailed until rebellion and pride came,
in the romantic era, to be admired for their own sake."

In Berlin's description, the people who initiated and
promoted the romantic movement "were not primarily

interested in knowledge or in the advance of science." The movement was driven by "a great turning towards emotionalism" and by "an outbreak of craving for the infinite." The romantics admired "wild genius, outlaws, heroes, aestheticism, self-destruction." Therefore, "common sense, moderation, was very far from their thoughts."

Emotionalism is a doctrine in both aesthetics and ethics, making emotions the measure of value in art and in conduct. Emotional intensity was the romantics' guiding star.

Emotional intensity characterizes the dream experience, as we have seen. The dream world lacks the "objective pattern" we know from the common-sense world of waking experience. By embracing emotional intensity and rejecting the belief in an objective pattern to the world, the romantics were making dreams, not reality, their touchstone – an astonishing development! This gives credence to Isaiah Berlin's bold claim that romanticism represented "the greatest single shift in the consciousness of the West that has occurred."

Berlin and other scholars have struggled to find a coherent account of romanticism or provide a clear definition. The great scholar A.O. Lovejoy is said to have been reduced almost to despair by his inability to bring order to the subject. Finally he concluded that he could not see any common thread linking all that had been associated with romanticism. Berlin reels off some examples from the vast range of characteristics that were said to define romanticism:

Romanticism is the primitive, the untutored, it is youth, the exuberant sense of life of the natural man, but it is also pallor, fever, disease, decadence, the maladie du siècle, *La Belle Dame Sans Merci, the Dance of Death, indeed Death itself. . . . It is the strange, the exotic, the grotesque, the mysterious, the supernatural, ruins, moonlight, enchanted castles, hunting horns, elves, giants, griffins, falling water, the old mill on the Floss, darkness and the powers of darkness, phantoms, vampires, nameless terror, the irrational, the unutterable.*

Berlin goes on at length in this vein, emphasizing the problem raised by the contradictions among these various examples of romanticism.

If we consider this list from the standpoint of the dream world, however, the problem disappears. After all, a scholar of dreams would not try to define the dream by accumulating many examples of dreams and searching for what they have in common. That would be absurd. The content of dreams would not reward such an approach. Rather, the dream world might best be defined in terms of what it lacks: an *objective order*. Similarly, romanticism is marked primarily by its turning away from objectivity.

"It was the Romantics," writes Bruce Fleming, "those grandfathers and –mothers of the modern world, who first rejected the notion of the representational window as [a] means out of the room of the self." They exalted subjectivity instead. In the new way of thinking that followed, "All inquiry, all thought, all academic enterprises – even science! only there, of course, the scientists demurred, but what did they know? – were subjective, or at least we could never achieve an objective world even if it turned out to exist."

The romantics believed they were rejecting the rationalism of the Enlightenment. They were, but they actually went much further. They rejected not only the continental Enlightenment with its emphasis on reason, but also the Scottish Enlightenment with its emphasis on common sense – the branch of the Enlightenment that greatly influenced the American Founders. Perhaps carried away by their reliance on emotionalism, the romantics broke with the idea that there is an objective, knowable pattern to the world.

By discarding objectivity and common sense, they opened the floodgates to waves of irrationalist doctrines: Hegelianism, Marxism, progressivism, existentialism, postmodernism, and all the rest.

Sense and Sensibility can again help our understanding here. Recall that Elinor and Marianne personify common sense and sensibility, respectively. But they do much more. Each does double duty, embodying also a turning of the great wheel of the ages – a phase in the transformation of European consciousness that Berlin discusses. Elinor personifies both common sense and the Enlightenment period. Marianne represents both sensibility and the romantic period, with all its emotionalism.

This broader significance has generally been missed by scholars. For example, Mark Schorer writes in his introduction to *Sense and Sensibility* that Jane Austen "very probably ... thought that she was writing small, modestly edifying comedies of contemporary manners, and nothing more." Read any literary authority on Austen and you will likely be told something similar. Schorer speaks for most experts when he considers the great convulsions in history that occurred during Jane Austen's lifetime and concludes that "none of these plays any part in her novels."

I believe that precisely the opposite is true of *Sense and Sensibility*. Here, Austen reaches us by means of our imagination – just as C. S. Lewis said that George Mac-Donald had done in his books of fantasy. Lewis wrote that MacDonald had baptized his imagination, preparing him for his intellectual assent to the truth of Christianity and his conversion. In like manner, Austen prepares us to understand a great historical change by presenting it in personal terms, in a story about two sisters.

When *Sense and Sensibility* was published in 1811, romanticism had been on the rise for about half a century, in Berlin's chronology. We can understand the story better by realizing that Austen intended Marianne to personify romanticism while Elinor represents common-sense realism. Thus when Elinor speaks of settling opinions on "the reasonable basis of common sense and observation," Austen is presenting the great themes of the common-sense Enlightenment's account of human understanding. In that account, common sense is the indispensable basis of understanding, while observation, including the rigorous form of observation made possible by the scientific method, is how we learn.

Similarly, we can view Marianne's close brush with death as more than a plot device. It reflects the self-destructive embrace of martyrdom that was central to romanticism from its beginning in Germany. Between the late 1760s and the early 1780s, Berlin writes, the idea of the romantic hero was taking hold of the German imagination. During this period, heroic martyrdom became "a quality to be worshipped for its own sake."

But heroic martyrdom appears in connection with an impulse to destroy one's surroundings, as Berlin explains:

This is the beginning of ... the Nietzschean figure who wishes to raze to the ground a society whose system of values is such that a superior person who truly understands what it is to be free cannot operate in terms of it, and therefore prefers to destroy it,... prefers self-destruction, suicide ....

This is very different from the religious concept of martyrdom in which no destruction is sought. Instead, Berlin's description of the romantic hero evokes the figure of Satan, propelled by a feeling of injured pride to lead a rebellion against heaven. It also describes Hitler, who exalted himself by whipping up Germany's injured pride, led Germany into wars of unimaginable destruction, brought Germany to ruin, and finally committed suicide.

Of course, the idea of razing society to the ground has no part in Austen's portrait of Marianne, but the author deftly shows us in miniature that an attraction to romanticism's heroic martyrdom is destructive of the individual. We are thus prepared to recognize that the spirit of heroic martyrdom would be destructive in a nation that worships it.

I N ELEVATING EMOTIONALISM over common sense, the romantics opened the door to the doctrines of irrationalism, which led in turn to a wider adoption of irrationality. The process took generations, but the irrationalism embraced by writers, artists, philosophers, and sophisticated elites gradually seeped down into the mindset of ordinary people.

George MacDonald Fraser offers a fascinating glimpse of how a common-sense frame of mind gave way to emotionalism. In *Quartered Safe Out Here: A Harrowing Tale of World War II,* he first recounts the time when soldiers in his army unit in Burma dealt with the deaths of two brothers-in-arms:

An outsider might have thought, mistakenly, that the section was unmoved by the deaths of Gale and Little. There was no outward show of sorrow, no reminiscences or eulogies.... It was part of war.... Whatever sorrow was felt, there was no point in talking or brooding about it, much less in making for form's sake, a parade of it....

... the resolve to conceal emotion which is not only embarrassing and useless, but harmful, is just plain common sense.

But that was half a century ago. Things are different now ....

To illustrate the subsequent cultural change – a change encouraged by the media, he says – Fraser gives the example of a response to the disaster at the Hillsborough stadium in Sheffield in April 1989, when ninety-six supporters of the Liverpool Football Club were crushed to death as a game was starting.

I knew a young Liverpudlian who, following the Hillsborough disaster, stayed away from work because, he said, of the grief he felt for those supporters of his team who had died on the terraces. He didn't know them, he hadn't been there, but he was too distressed to work.... One shouldn't be too hard on the young man; he had been conditioned to believe that it was right, even proper, to indulge his emotions; he probably felt virtuous for having done so.

By contrast, the soldiers in Fraser's section had more reason for grief, but were able to contain their emotions. They held on to common sense in order to survive – just as Austen's Marianne is able to find her way to a secure footing in common sense, and live.

But the process of abandoning common sense is now far advanced in America too. Or rather, it is not simply being abandoned, but is under a radical attack, and this assault is having an effect on the lives of average people.

IMPOSING AN ALTERNATIVE
TO COMMON SENSE

The dogma of the intellectual upper classes today is a bed-rock belief in what I call "linguistic realism" .... If I say I am a woman, I am a woman, whatever others think. If I say I feel myself to be oppressed, I am. If I say that I was the victim of what we call sexual assault, I am — even if a court later decides there was no assault and hence no victim.

BRUCE FLEMING
"Dogma of the Day"

ORDINARY AMERICANS ARE, for the most part, still common-sense realists. Like Abraham Lincoln, they know that even if you call a tail a leg, it's still a tail. For most people, especially those who have not been steeped in sophisticated Ivy League thinking, it is equally self-evident that a boy in a tutu and a tiara is a boy even if he claims to be female. But for our progressive elite, what the boy *says* must now determine which bathroom and shower facility he may use. The ruling class in and out of government is trying to impose *linguistic realism* on ordinary people, by official edicts and by social pressure.

As you no doubt already know, this does not stop with boys who insist they are girls, or vice versa. In

2016, for example, New York City's Commission on Human Rights released a list of thirty-one recognized genders, or "gender identities," that are deemed to merit legal protection. The list includes "drag king," "drag queen," "butch," "femme queen," "gender fluid," "gender blender," "gender gifted," "gender bender," and "femme person of transgender experience." Businesses can now be fined as much as $250,000 for refusing to address someone by his or her preferred pronoun. In addition, New Yorkers may use the bathroom or locker room of their choice according to "gender identity," without having to show any kind of documentation or proof that they really are what they claim but don't appear to be.

In a world governed by linguistic realism, what people say about themselves and others has more reality than any objective facts. "The basis of linguistic realism," writes Bruce Fleming, "is the rejection of words as a means, and the acceptance of them, and other forms of representation, as an end in themselves." That is why we are no longer taught to say "words can never hurt me," but instead we hear about the menace of "hate speech." We are told that "speech is violence."

The split between the common-sense realism of regular Americans and the linguistic realism and political correctness championed by the sophisticated members of the progressive elite goes a long way toward explaining the current divide between average Americans and elites. America has always had an elite, but America has not always had this divide. It used to be that elite Americans and ordinary Americans alike were common-sense realists. The Founders were masters of the formal philosophy of common-sense realism, and for generations the education of elite Americans was grounded in common-sense realism.

THE ABANDONMENT OF common-sense realism did not happen because it was disproved. For that matter, philosophers including Karl Popper have made the case that it cannot be disproved – which is not to say that it can be proved either, much as the common-sense reality that a carafe cannot at the same time be a woman is not subject to either proof or disproof.

We might demonstrate that some notions are contrary to common sense: that they are likely to result in serious harm, for example. Indeed, people cannot thoroughly abandon common sense in the conduct of their daily lives without putting their safety or survival at risk. But in some areas of life – such as in movies and novels, in philosophy, and even, far too often, in political discourse – nonsense can run unchecked by contact with reality.

An interesting example in fiction is the "magic realism" of Gabriel García Márquez. A man of the Left and a friend of Fidel Castro, García Márquez was awarded the Nobel Prize in Literature, largely for his enormously influential novel *One Hundred Years of Solitude*, published in 1967. As you might guess, magic realism is not constrained by what we know through common sense to be real. Here is what magic realism looks like in the novel:

As soon as José Arcadio closed the bedroom door the sound of a pistol shot echoed through the house. A trickle of blood came out under the door, crossed the living room, went out into the street, continued on in a straight line across the uneven terraces, went down steps and climbed over curbs, passed along the Street of the Turks, turned a corner to the right and another to the left, made a right angle at the Buendía house, went in under the closed door, crossed through the parlor, hugging the walls so as not to stain the rugs, went on to the other living room, made a wide curve to avoid the dining-room table, went along the porch with the begonias, and passed without being seen under Amaranta's chair as she gave an arithmetic lesson to Aureliano José, and went through the pantry and came out in the kitchen, where Úrsula was getting ready to crack thirty-six eggs to make bread.

Márquez really pounds away against common-sense reality, doesn't he?

Nonsense in literature is one thing, but in other domains there are more serious consequences to rejecting common sense. And those who champion linguistic realism and magic realism are part of a relentless campaign against common sense, attacking it wherever possible. The result has been a general weakening of the claims of common sense in the West.

MISUNDERSTANDING EINSTEIN

At the beginning of the 1920s the belief began to circulate, for the first time at a popular level, that there were no longer any absolutes: of time and space, of good and evil, of knowledge, above all of value. Mistakenly but perhaps inevitably, relativity became confused with relativism.

PAUL JOHNSON
Modern Times

MANY PEOPLE HAVE been eager to overthrow common sense and celebrate its fall, but part of the story began with a tragic misunderstanding. While romanticism opened the door to irrationalist doctrines that rebelled against common sense, a further assault came with the relentless promotion of relativism in every aspect of modern life, backed by the supposed authority of science. In particular, it was the power of Albert Einstein's astonishing celebrity that enabled relativism to spread in the popular imagination.

This cultural development resulted from a misunderstanding of what Einstein had found. The basic error was to confuse *relativity*, which means one thing changing in relation to another, with *relativism*, which is the absence of absolute values. But even the emphasis on "relativity" gets Einstein wrong. What he actually discovered was an *invariance,* and in fact he considered naming his theory "the invariance theory." Einstein demonstrated that the speed of light in a vacuum – the "c" in the equation $E = mc^2$ – is a constant.

As you know, light does not behave like matter with respect to acceleration. If a projectile is fired from a rocket ship traveling at great speed, the velocity of the projectile will vary according to the speed of the rocket ship and the direction of the projectile in relation to that of the rocket ship. Fired in the direction the ship is traveling, the velocity of the projectile will be greater than if it were fired in the opposite direction. But if you aimed a powerful light beam in any direction relative to the movement of the ship, it would travel at exactly the same velocity, because the speed of light is constant.

Huston Smith, in his book *Beyond the Post-Modern Mind,* makes the point that the "invariance" that Einstein discovered is "more fundamental than the relativities it explains," but this fact has been obscured by an unfortunate choice of terms:

In calling his epochal discovery "relativity" Einstein all but named our age, which is riddled with relativities of unbelievable variety, but what he actually unearthed was its opposite: invariance – the constancy of light's speed despite the apparent confusions, illusions, and contradictions produced by the relative motions or actions of gravity.

Calling his discovery the "invariance theory" would have been more accurate, as Smith observes.

It would also have had a much different resonance in

the public mind. Moreover, the "relativities" in the equation have nothing to say about the existence of truth or unchanging values. The notion that science endorses relativism thus arose from a deep misunderstanding of Einstein's work.

"No one was more distressed than Einstein by this public misapprehension," writes Paul Johnson. Einstein, in fact, "believed passionately in absolute standards of right and wrong. His professional life was devoted to the quest not only for truth but for certitude." To his dismay, Einstein "lived to see moral relativism, to him a disease, become a social pandemic."

More generally, the idea that all truth is subjective began to spread. But a philosophy of relativism – a belief that no objective truth exists – cannot withstand scrutiny. Relativism posits that there is no such thing as truth, yet we have seen the existence of common-sense truths that are beyond challenge. People who try to challenge the truth that tables cannot sing or that we ordinary mortals cannot walk on water will quickly run into problems. These truths aren't budging no matter how hard the relativist tries to move them.

The central claim of relativism, then, is self-evidently false. It is also self-refuting. Relativism declares it to be *true* that there is no such thing as truth, but this claim obviously contradicts itself. Relativism thus fails for the simple reason that it is absurd.

Yet relativism has increased its hold on the popular imagination, and consequently the standing of common sense has diminished. Even so, joining in or succumbing to the campaign against common sense is a choice.

We have the option of doing what people have always been able to do: make the life-defining effort to become a person of robust common sense. Here is how Lionel Trilling describes one such person:

He is indifferent to the allurements of elaborate theory or of extreme sensibility. The medium of his thought is common sense, and his commitment to intellect is fortified by an old-fashioned faith that the truth can be got at, that we can, if we actually want to, see the object as it really is.

Trilling is brilliantly describing George Orwell in this passage. But what is fascinating about the description is how generic it also is. It could be the description of any person who is well along the common-sense path to wisdom.

SUGGESTIONS FOR FURTHER READING

Robert Curry, *Common Sense Nation: Unlocking the Forgotten Power of the American Idea*, Encounter Books, 2015 – In this companion volume I explore the impact of common-sense thinking on the American founding.

Thomas Paine, *Common Sense*, 1776 – This little book put common sense to work, igniting the American Revolution.

Jane Austen, *Sense and Sensibility*, 1811 – This delightful novel brings common sense to life.

Arthur Herman, *How the Scots Invented the Modern World: The True Story of How Western Europe's Poorest Nation Created Our World and Everything in It*, Crown Publishers, 2001 – This fascinating book is a joy to read. Highly recommended.

John Tamny, *Popular Economics*, Regnery Publishing, 2015 – You could also call it *Common Sense Economics*.

Giovanni B. Grandi, editor, *Thomas Reid: Selected Philosophical Writings*, Imprint Academic, 2012 – A magnificent resource for the philosophically inclined, it makes Reid's common-sense realism accessible to modern readers.

Many thanks to my awesome editor, Carol Staswick, and to all the other wonderful folks at Encounter Books.

INDEX

Alzheimer's disease, 35

American Revolution, 19, 80, 81–82

Anna Karenina (Tolstoy), 39, 43–44, 66

As I Lay Dying (Faulkner), 40

Austen, Jane, 61, 62–65; on prudence, 67–69; and Reid, 71–72; on romanticism, 90–91, 94

Bateson, Gregory, 49

Berlin, Isaiah, 87–89

Beyond the Post-Modern Mind (Smith), 100

Brief History of Time, A (Hawking), 49

Castro, Fidel, 97

Catton, Bruce, 17

Civil War, 17

coma, 35–36

Common Sense Nation (Curry), 19–20, 72

common-sense realism, 25–28, 95, 96–97; Reid on, 29–31

Constitution of the United States, 19, 24

Cuba, 80

Darwin, Charles, 76

Declaration of Independence, 19, 27

Descartes, René, 45–47

dreams, 39–41, 88, 89

economics, 76, 80, 83–85

Einstein, Albert, 50–51, 99–101

Emerson, Ralph Waldo, 52

Enlightenment, 87, 90–91

Essay on the History of Civil Society, An (Ferguson), 75

evolution, 76; social, 74–77

existentialism, 25, 90

Faulkner, William, 40

Ferguson, Adam, 74–75, 76

Fingarette, Herbert, 55

Fleming, Bruce, 89, 95, 96

Founders, 19–21; common-sense realism of, 27–28, 31, 96–97; and Scottish Enlightenment, 90; on self-evident truths, 27, 41, 72, 73–74,

Fraser, George MacDonald, 93–94

Freud, Sigmund, 55–56

Galileo Galilei, 50

García Márquez, Gabriel, 97–98

gender identity, 24, 95–96

government inefficiency, 82–85

Grant, Ulysses S., 17–18, 19

Guelzo, Allen, 25, 31

INDEX

hate speech, 96
Hawking, Stephen, 49
Hegelianism, 25, 90
Herman, Arthur, 25, 26–27, 29, 30
Hillsborough stadium disaster, 93–94
Hitler, Adolf, 92

Inquiry into the Human Mind on the Principles of Common Sense, An (Reid), 29–31, 43, 68–69
Islamophobia, 24

Jaffa, Harry, 73–74
James, William, 52–54
Jefferson, Thomas, 23, 27, 73–74
Johnson, Paul, 99, 101

Kepler, Johannes, 50

language: capacity for, 19; development of, 45, 75–76
Lee, Ang, 62
Lewis, C. S., 69, 87, 91
Lincoln, Abraham, 27, 95
linguistic realism, 95–96
Lovejoy, A. O., 88
Love's Executioner and Other Tales of Psychiatry (Yalom), 56–57

MacDonald, George, 91
magic realism, 97–98
Mao Zedong, 79
Marcuse, Herbert, 79
Marx, Karl, 79, 80
Marxism, 25, 79–81, 90
McClellan, George, 17
Mind and Nature (Bateson), 49–51
Modern Times (Johnson), 99
multiculturalism, 26, 28

Natural Right and History (Strauss), 47–48
New Birth of Freedom, A (Jaffa), 73–74
New Left, 79
Newton, Isaac, 50
New York City Commission on Human Rights, 96
North Korea, 80

One Hundred Years of Solitude (García Márquez), 97–98
O'Rourke, P. J., 33–34, 57, 61, 82
Orwell, George, 102

Paine, Thomas, 23
Parliament of Whores (O'Rourke), 33
phobia, 55–56
Pluto, 53
political correctness, 24, 26, 28
Popper, Karl, 49–50, 51, 97
postmodernism, 25, 90
Preface to Paradise Lost, A (Lewis), 87
progressivism, 25, 90
prudence, 67–68
psychiatric disorder, 36–37
psychotherapy, 55–59

Quartered Safe Out Here (Fraser), 93–94

Reid, Thomas, 29–31, 41; on Descartes, 46–47; on language, 43; moral concern of, 68–69; on prudence, 71; on self-evident truth, 30–31, 72
relativism, 28, 51, 99–101
relativity (theory of), 50–51, 99–101
Ridley, Matt, 75

romanticism, 25, 87–92; in Austen, 63–65, 61, 90–92; heroic martyrdom in, 91–92; subjectivity in, 88–89

Roots of Romanticism, The (Berlin), 87–89

Saudi Arabia, 81
Schorer, Mark, 90–91
Schuon, Frithjof, 46
science, 47–48; and common sense, 49–54; theory & falsifiability in, 49–51
self-evident truth, 27, 30–31, 41; and Descartes, 46; discovery of, 72–74
self-government, 28, 71–72
Self in Transformation, The (Fingarette), 55
Sense and Sensibility (Austen), 61, 62–65, 61–63; prudence in,

67–69; Enlightenment vs. romanticism in, 90–92; self-mastery in, 71–72
Sense and Sensibility (film), 62, 65
Smith, Huston, 100
Soviet Union, 80
Strauss, Leo, 47–48
student revolution (1960s), 26

Tolstoy, Leo, 39, 43–44, 66
Trilling, Lionel, 102
Truffaut, François, 18

Veterans Health Administration, 84–85

Wild Child, The (Truffaut), 18
World War II, 93

Yalom, Irvin, 56–58

RECLAIMING COMMON SENSE *has been set in Bell, a type based on designs Richard Austin cut in 1788 for John Bell's British Type Foundry. Intended for an unrealized edition of* The Book of Common Prayer, *the type enjoyed its first significant success in Bell's daily newspaper,* The Oracle. *Although classed as a modern face by Stanley Morison, Bell (to quote Alexander Lawson) "is a more faithful rendition of the transitional styles.... Certainly the design is closer to Baskerville ... than to the so-called classic romans of Bodoni and Didot." Among Bell's most notable features are its tapered serifs, a radical contrast to the bracketed serifs of English types of the era — like Caslon — and to the European types John Bell studied as models. The types were quite popular in the United States in the early nineteenth century, but were swiftly overshadowed by types based on Austin's later designs, that is, the "Scotch" romans. Bell began to return to favor toward the end of the century, appearing in the work of influential American designers like D. B. Updike and Bruce Rogers — despite being available solely for hand composition. It was not until 1930 that the types were finally cut for machine composition by the Monotype Corporation under Morison's direction, making this handsome face available for general book work and ensuring its continued popularity.*

DESIGN & COMPOSITION BY CARL W. SCARBROUGH